A MATTER OF PERSPECTIVE

S. JONES-MARSHALL

BALBOA.
PRESS
A DIVISION OF HAY HOUSE

Balboa Press books may be ordered through booksellers or by contacting:

Balboa Press
A Division of Hay House
1663 Liberty Drive
Bloomington, IN 47403
www.balboapress.com
1 (877) 407-4847

Print information available on the last page.

ISBN: 978-1-5043-7165-0 (sc)
ISBN: 978-1-5043-7201-5 (e)

Balboa Press rev. date: 12/14/2016

Contents

Choosing

Choosing to live or die
Is all up to that person
Sometimes it's a matter
Of give and take

For life
Is what you make of it
And you can't blame
Anyone for the chooses you've made

Living

Living to die
Is all a process
We all follow

Because we realize
That our time
Here is just
A blink of the eye

When you consider
What waits for us
In glory when this life is over

What

What this life
Has to offer
Cannot be out weighed
By what we have in store

When we reach
The promise land
We will know
Nothing but joy

A shame

There are times
In which we do things
That we are ashamed of

It is in these times
That we must humble our hearts
And ask for forgiveness

Learn

We learn
How to cope
When things
Don't go our way

It is hard to learn
Because our minds
Are not wired that way

Joy

We can find joy
In the things we do

The only trick
Is to transform you mind
Into that of a child

Love

Love is a splendid thing
Because it teaches us
Something about ourselves

Because we must be
Totally open to it
And not run away from it

When we do
We miss out
On the greatest experience
We can have

Differences

We all have differences
It could be the color of our skin
Or the language we speak

Some differences
Can be seen or heard

Those there are those differences
That can escape
The normal senses

People seem to shy away
From the things
That they do not understand

Looking

People are looking
At our lives
To compare
Where they should be

Though there are
Different places we should be

Just because I'm at one place
Doesn't mean that
They should be
Where I'm at

Seeing

Seeing my life
At this time
Makes me regret
Some of the decisions I've made

Though there are
Some things I'm proud of
Like writing this poem
For others to read

Waking

I'm waking these feelings
Once more
To reach out
In hope and love

To share
A piece of my heart
So you can come in

And dwell there a while
So we can learn
From each other

When

When we learn
That true growth
Means there
Will be pain

Though when we realize
That this growth
Will help to shape us
Into a shining light

Laughter

Laughter is the greatest gift
That we have
Because it
Can brighten a dark day

It's something
That lifts a broken spirit
And puts a smile on your face

Night

In the night
There is peace
In the night
There is love

We can find
True solitude
In the darkness

In the night
There is peace
In the night
There is love

Great expression
Of love
Are found in the darkness

In the night
There is peace
In the night
There is love

Faith

Faith
Is something unseen
Faith
Is a feeling

When we have faith
We know

There is something
Greater than our understand

Faith
Is something unseen
Faith
Is a feeling

Our faith
Maybe small

But He know
Our hearts and minds

Faith
Is something unseen
Faith
Is a feeling

Understanding

Our understanding
Is ever changing
Because what we know now
Can change in a matter of minutes
So our understanding
Has to grow and shape
The situation we're in

Facts

The facts of life
Are a guide
To what life
May hold for us

We learn early on
What society expects

And what they frown on
Because of their ignorance
On the subject

Writing

Writing is a wonderful thing
Because it can enhance
Our understanding of something

It is also an outlet
For feelings
That cannot be spoken

Wrapped

You've wrapped my heart
In love so secure
You've wrapped my heart
So it can not break

I've never known someone
That gave love completely

Without hesitation
To someone like me

You've wrapped my heart
In love so secure
You've wrapped my heart
So it can not break

I've had my heart broken
Many times before

Though you've told me
That you're never letting go

You've wrapped my heart
In love so secure
You've wrapped my heard
So it can not break

Looking

Looking at the snow
As it falls gently to earth
Looking at the snow
As it covers everything

The memories
That it brings back

Of earlier times
When I could play

Looking at the snow
As it falls gently to earth
Looking at the snow
As it covers everything

Sledding on hills
Is where I wish I could be

Building a snowman
And having snow balls fights

Looking at the snow
As it falls gently to earth
Looking at the snow
As it covers everything

Everyone

Everyone
Fights for position
Everyone
Struggles to be heard

In the chaos of our world
Things get over looked
And this means people too

Everyone
Fights for position
Everyone
Struggles to be heard

When we feel
That nothing is going right
We stand on tip toe
And shout with all our might

Everyone
Fights for position
Everyone
Struggles to be heard

Inside

When we look
Inside ourselves
We find
All our hopes and dreams

We realize
That our hopes and dream
May never be fulfilled
But we strive to make them come true

Ourselves

We think we know
Ourselves
But this is not true
Because of society

Society likes to label us
And that label sometimes sticks

We begin to think
We are that label
And nothing else

But society
Is wrong
Just because you're different
That label
Does not define who you are

Others

We have a way
Of listening to others
Going by what they say

This can be dangerous
Because we may loose
Who we are

Paperwork

All we seem to do is paperwork
When we go to a doctor
There is paperwork

Our lives have become so busy
That we find ourselves
Doing paperwork for everything

When we take a vacation
We think we get away from it
But we still do it
Without thinking

When we get back from vacation
You can't believe
The pile of paperwork
On your desk
Just calling your name
We never get away from paperwork

Regret

We regret things we've done
Or things we've said

It's not an easy thing
To admit to ourselves
And admitting them
To others is even harder

Though we learn
That we have trouble
Living with regrets on our hearts

Being Handy Capable

Being handy capable
Is a choice
Being handy capable
Should be a way of life

Some individuals
With a disability

Get so caught up
In what society says
They give up
Before they ever start

Being handy capable
Is a choice
Being handy capable
Should be a way of life

Some people think
That someone with a disability
Cannot contribute to society

Though I would care to differ
Because these individuals
Can sometimes do more for society
Than anyone thinks

Being handy capable
Is a choice
Being handy capable
Should be a way of life

Being

The state of being is complicated
Because of what the world dictates

We often times conform
To the things of this world

When all along
We should be mindful
Of what we think and feel

Working

Working is what we do
From the day we are born

The way we work to start
Is by learning about our surroundings

As we age and go to school
The work we do is still by learning our surroundings
Though we are also learning of others surroundings

When we reach adulthood
We start getting paid for our work
Though we think we have stopped learning

But we never really stop learnning
We stop learning when we die

Lives

Our lives
Are nothing but a grain of sand
When you think of the universe

Our bodies
Are constantly changing
In ways most people don't notice

Along

When you think
The day you were born
You agreed to start an adventure
And therefore come along for the ride

You don't really know
Where you're going

You have an idea
Of your final destination
But you never truly know
Where this ride will stop

Endings

Beginnings and endings
Is what life is about

We learn how to live
Because of this beginnings and endings
We realize in these times

We can either learn to grow
Or we can
Let these times pass us by

Society

Society
Is moving too fast
Society
Never allows for change

As we move
Along this road of life

We are made aware
Of the problems being presented

Society
Is moving too fast
Society
Never allows for change

People is the public eye
Have the most trouble
When things around them change

Society
Is moving too fast
Society
Never allows for change

Hopeful

I am hopeful
For another sun rise
I am hopeful
For another sun set

We realize
That these things
Are not guaranteed

Finally

I've finally realized
That things
Are as good
As they are going to get

When

When time is short
And you have used
Every last bit of self-control
To hold yourself together

There is one greater
That yearns for your call
So He can help you
In whatever way you need

His name is Jesus Christ
And He will help
In every situation

All you have to do
Is call upon His name
And He will never leave your side

A Friendship

A Friendship is a unique relationship
It gives us what we need at that moment
A Friendship gives us strength
In the depth of our sorrow
A friendship can make us fly

When we feel
That no one cares

And we feel
That the load is too much
For us to carry

Our minds are transformed
By this relationship
Because we know someone does care
Which lightens our load

A Friendship is a unique relationship
It gives us what we need at that moment
A Friendship gives us strength
In the depth of our sorrow
A friendship can make us fly

In our darkest moments
When we cannot go on

It is our friends
That help us to see
The light at the end of the tunnel

A Friendship is a unique relationship
It gives us what we need at that moment
A Friendship gives us strength
In the depth of our sorrow
A friendship can make us fly

As The Tears

As the tears
Flow down my face
As the tears
Fall I feel relief

Every emotion
Keeps building up inside of me

To the point
Of total collapse

As the tears
Flow down my face
As the tears
Fall I feel relief

The tears sting my eyes
And I feel helpless

The tears stain within
Where no one can see what is left

As the tears
Flow down my face
As the tears
Fall I feel relief

Came

When I came alive
Was when you came into my life
When I came alive
There was nothing, but joy in my life

For years I searched for love
And I never found it

There were times that I thought I'd found it
But to my surprise it was nothing
But my need to have someone

When I came alive
Was when you came into my life
When I came alive
There was nothing, but joy in my life

Why is love to illusive
When we think we've found it
It just turns out to be a mistake

But when you really do find it
There is nothing to describe the peace you feel

When I came alive
Was when you came into my life
When I came alive
There was nothing, but joy in my life

Dealing with Death

Dealing with death
Is never easy
Dealing with death
Is like waves in the ocean

When our loved ones pass over to the other side
It leaves a great hole where they once stood

We know that the hole will never be filled again
Though if we can concentrate on
our memories of them
We find that the darkness of the hole
Is magically filled with the light of their love

Dealing with Death
Is never easy
Dealing with Death
Is like waves of the ocean

We learn in life
That our family is what has made us
Who and what we are

When a family member passes
We feel great loss
But if we believe in Jesus Christ
We know that we will see them again
When the waves wash us back into the ocean

Dealing with Death
Is never easy
Dealing with Death
Is like waves of the ocean

Final Gift

My final gift to you
Is nothing compared to the gift you gave me
When you decided to call me a friend
Which in reality is what changed my life
Knowing that even though you are gone
I can still lean on your guidance and wisdom
For the rest of my life

Do Not Be Afraid

My child
Do not be afraid
Because I've already numbered the hairs of your head
And I'll be with you until the end

Do not be dismayed
When the path you're on
Gets hilly
Because I'm there leading the way

My child
I'll be waiting for you
For you on the other side

Dying Inside

Dying inside
Because of being afraid
Dying inside
Because there is no hope

Living within constraints
Is not really living

But we all learn
That we must do this

Dying inside
Because of being afraid
Dying inside
Because there is no hope

To be able to be open
With how you feel is wonderful

The only fall back to this
Is to have the person laugh in your face

And tell you that they
Could never feel that way about you

Dying inside
Because of being afraid
Dying inside
Because there is no hope

Enough

When is enough, enough
When you've been knocked down for the third time
When is enough, enough
When you have to
Relearn to walk for the third time

When life seems
To be set against you

And the further you get up the ladder
Is when you realize
How much longer the ladder is getting

When is enough, enough
When you've been knocked down for the third time
When is enough, enough
When you have to
Relearn to walk for the third time

It is at this time
You realize

You can either
Face the challenge
And overcome it

Or you can allow yourself
To be beat by it
And allow the special person
You are inside die

When is enough, enough
When you've been knocked down for the third time
When is enough, enough
When you have to
Relearn to walk for the third time

Fear

Living in fear
That your secret will come out
Living in fear
That you can't be honest

In society
Feeling in a way

That is not accepted by society
Can cause you great distress

Living in fear
That your secret will come out
Living in fear
That you can't be honest

When you have to hide
The person you truly are

Causes you great heart break
Because having to hide
Who you are
Wears heavy on your heart

Living in fear
That your secret will come out
Living in fear
That you can't be honest

Find

When you are injured
And you happen to find someone
That you feel goes out of their way
To make sure that you feel safe
That person becomes a friend

When you can't wait
To work with them again

Because you know
That everything will be done rght
And your safety is the first thing
That they think of calms your mind

When you are injured
And you happen to find someone
That you feel goes out of their way
To make sure that you feel safe
That person becomes a friend

It takes a special person
To do that kind of work

And they are few and far between
But when you find someone like that
You should try and maintain
The friendship no matter what

When you are injured
And you happen to find someone
It seems they go out of their way
To make sure that you feel safe
That person becomes a friend

Finding

Finding love
Is never easy
Finding love
Can take a lifetime

When I found you
My mind couldn't handle anymore

Though you swept into my life
And for that I'll always be grateful

Finding love
Is never easy
Finding love
Can take a lifetime

Since you
Came into my life

My heart has known contentment
And you've lightened my load

Finding love
Is never easy
Finding love
Can take a lifetime

Finding

Finding
Your hearts desire
Finding
Life's true meaning

We live in a world
Where everything is hidden

People hide their emotions
To keep from getting hurt
And they're scared
To let anyone see the real them

Finding
Your hearts desire
Finding
Life's true meaning

The meaning
Of life
Is different for everyone

Because we each treasure something different
But when we realize

That people are the treasures
We should be concerned with
Life takes on a different meaning
And we will realize we have discovered
The true meaning of life

When you find
Your hearts desire
You will have peace
When you find
That helping someone
Is the meaning of life!

Friendships

Friendships are like sand in an hour glass
Moving ever so slowly as it falls
Friendships are like waves of the ocean
Licking the sands as the tide comes in

We cannot predict
The amount of time
We will have with someone

Or the direction
The friendship will go

Friendships are like sand in an hour glass
Moving ever so slowly as it falls
Friendships are like waves of the ocean
Licking the sands as the tide comes in

We must cherish
Every second we have with the person

Because we don't know
When the tide
May wash them out of our lives

Friendships are like sand in an hour glass
Moving ever so slowly as it falls
Friendships are like waves of the ocean
Licking the sands as the tide comes in

Holding On

Holding on
To an idea
Holding on
To something that may not even be there

There are so many
Things in this life

That seem so unfair
Even though we know this
We can't help but feeling a certain way

Holding on
To an idea
Holding on
To something that may not even be there

When we fall in love
We hope that the other person
Feels about us the same way

But there is no guarantee
That anything will happen

But we hope with everything
That they may

Holding on
To an idea
Holding on
To something that may not even be there

Images

Some of the images I have
Are of a much happier time
Some of the images I have
Are of times I wish I could forget

Of me as a child
Make me feel happy

No one ever said life was easy
Because as I grew
Things in my life changed

Though as I grew the images changed
Because of things that had happened
Some of the images locked in my head
We won't even discuss

When you entered my life
You started helping me create new images

Ones of happiness and hope
Ones that show the beauty of our love

You have helped me restore
The images I have in my head
And you've helped me understand

The things of the past
Are dead and forgotten

But the images
That we are creating now
Are of the life that we are going to have together

Some of the images I have
Are to be held on to and cherished
Though some of the images I have
Are to be sat by the road and forgotten
Because all those images do are hold me down

Life

Life is a book
Filled with different stories
Though my book was missing a story
That only you could write
And with that story
You helped my heart to heal

During this journey
That we are all on

People drift in and out
Of our lives all the time
But the truly special ones
Leave a special mark on your heart
That leaves an echo of their presence

Life is a book
Filled with different stories
Though my book was missing a story
That only you could write
And with that story
You helped my heart to heal

I am so glad
That you drifted into my life

And have decided
To continue on this journey
With me until our journeys are complete

Life is a book
Filled with different stories
Though my book was missing a story
That only you could write
And with that story
You helped my heart

Listening

Listening
To all the voice around you
Listening
To what is being said

The art of listening
Is a very valuable tool

Because it can help
Keep you from making a fool of yourself

Listening
To all the voice around you
Listening
To what is being said

Though what is being said
Is not always in words

That is what makes
Understanding what people mean
When they act one way
But mean something totally different

Listening
To all the voice around you
Listening
To what is being said

Looking

Looking at my life
Before there was you
There was no reason for me to smile

Looking at my life
Since you became part of it
A smile has never left my face

You are now a part of my world
And something I cannot live without
Because looking at you
Allows me to know I've found the one

Looking

Looking inside
You will find out who you are
Looking inside
Will help you understand
Why you feel the way you do

During this journey
You will find your inner strength

It is during these times
That things may look their worst

Looking inside
You will find out who you are
Looking inside
Will help you understand
Why you feel the way you do

You will find
That even with love
You have to protect your heart

Though there are times
That you have to gamble it all
Because the rewards can be the greatest

Looking inside
You will find out who you are
Looking inside
Will help you understand
Why you feel the way you do

Lost

Lost
In a sea of guilt
Lost
In the valley of my own depression

When love finally found me
I didn't know how to accept it

Because it was something foreign to me
And I didn't know how to react

Lost
In a sea of guilt
Lost
In a valley of my own depression

Love

Looking through
The eyes of love
Feeling truly at ease
Being wrapped in pure love

When someone sees you
Through the eyes of love

They see you as a real person
And want nothing more than to love you

Looking through
The eyes of love
Feeling truly at ease
Being wrapped in pure love

As people walk into and out of our lives
We wonder how long they will be there

Because some people drift into our lives for a season
And others for a reason
But the true goal is

To find someone
That completes us

Looking through
The eyes of love
Feeling truly at ease
Being wrapped in pure love

When you find that special someone
You will know it
And you will both be able
To a long overdue sigh

Looking through
The eyes of love
Feeling truly at ease
Being wrapped in pure love

Printed in the United States
By Bookmasters